Pet Photo

Pet Name: _____
Birthday: _____
Male/Female: _____
Breed/Color: _____

Owner: _____
Address: _____
Phone: _____

Vet Hospital: _____
Veterinarian: _____
Phone: _____

Other Important Information

Spayed / Neutered: _____
Microchip #: _____
Allergies: _____
Medication Rx: _____

Flea/Tick Rx: _____
Groomer: _____
Pet Sitter: _____

Boarding: _____
Emergency Vet: _____
Other: _____
_____
_____
_____

Vaccination Record

Vaccination	Date	Brand	Serial #

Veterinary Visit Journal
Date: _____

Reason for Visit:
_____
_____
_____
_____
_____
_____
_____

What Veterinarian said about my pet:
_____
_____
_____
_____
_____
_____
_____

Tests Done:
_____
_____
_____
_____
_____

Medications:
_____
_____
_____
_____
_____

Diagnosis:

Recheck:

Pet Behavior Journal

Veterinary Visit Journal
Date: _____

Reason for Visit:
_____
_____
_____
_____
_____
_____

What Veterinarian said about my pet:
_____
_____
_____
_____
_____
_____

Tests Done:
_____
_____
_____
_____
_____

Medications:
_____
_____
_____
_____
_____

Diagnosis:

Recheck:

Pet Behavior Journal

Veterinary Visit Journal
Date: _____

Reason for Visit:
_____
_____
_____
_____
_____
_____
_____

What Veterinarian said about my pet:
_____
_____
_____
_____
_____
_____
_____

Tests Done:
_____
_____
_____
_____
_____

Medications:
_____
_____
_____
_____
_____

Diagnosis:

Recheck:

Pet Behavior Journal

Veterinary Visit Journal
Date: _____

Reason for Visit:
_____
_____
_____
_____
_____
_____
_____

What Veterinarian said about my pet:
_____
_____
_____
_____
_____
_____
_____

Tests Done:
_____
_____
_____
_____
_____

Medications:
_____
_____
_____
_____
_____

Diagnosis:

Recheck:

Pet Behavior Journal

Veterinary Visit Journal
Date: _____

Reason for Visit:
_____
_____
_____
_____
_____
_____

What Veterinarian said about my pet:
_____
_____
_____
_____
_____
_____

Tests Done:
_____
_____
_____
_____
_____

Medications:
_____
_____
_____
_____
_____

Diagnosis:

Recheck:

Pet Behavior Journal

Veterinary Visit Journal
Date: _____

Reason for Visit:
_____
_____
_____
_____
_____
_____
_____

What Veterinarian said about my pet:
_____
_____
_____
_____
_____
_____
_____

Tests Done:	Medications:
_____	_____
_____	_____
_____	_____
_____	_____
_____	_____
Diagnosis:	**Recheck:**

Pet Behavior Journal

Veterinary Visit Journal

Date: _____

Reason for Visit:
_____
_____
_____
_____
_____
_____
_____

What Veterinarian said about my pet:
_____
_____
_____
_____
_____
_____
_____

Tests Done:
_____
_____
_____
_____
_____

Medications:
_____
_____
_____
_____
_____

Diagnosis:

Recheck:

Pet Behavior Journal

Veterinary Visit Journal
Date: _____

Reason for Visit:
_____
_____
_____
_____
_____
_____
_____
_____

What Veterinarian said about my pet:
_____
_____
_____
_____
_____
_____
_____
_____

Tests Done:	Medications:
_____	_____
_____	_____
_____	_____
_____	_____
_____	_____

Diagnosis:	Recheck:

Pet Behavior Journal

Veterinary Visit Journal
Date: _____

Reason for Visit:
_____
_____
_____
_____
_____
_____
_____

What Veterinarian said about my pet:
_____
_____
_____
_____
_____
_____
_____

Tests Done:	Medications:
_____	_____
_____	_____
_____	_____
_____	_____
_____	_____

Diagnosis:	Recheck:

Pet Behavior Journal

Veterinary Visit Journal
Date: _____

Reason for Visit:
_____
_____
_____
_____
_____
_____
_____

What Veterinarian said about my pet:
_____
_____
_____
_____
_____
_____
_____

Tests Done:
_____
_____
_____
_____
_____
_____

Medications:
_____
_____
_____
_____
_____
_____

Diagnosis:

Recheck:

Pet Behavior Journal

Veterinary Visit Journal
Date: _____

Reason for Visit:
_____
_____
_____
_____
_____
_____
_____

What Veterinarian said about my pet:
_____
_____
_____
_____
_____
_____
_____
_____

Tests Done:	Medications:
_____	_____
_____	_____
_____	_____
_____	_____
_____	_____

Diagnosis:	Recheck:

Pet Behavior Journal

Veterinary Visit Journal
Date: _____

Reason for Visit:
_____
_____
_____
_____
_____
_____
_____

What Veterinarian said about my pet:
_____
_____
_____
_____
_____
_____
_____

Tests Done:	Medications:
_____	_____
_____	_____
_____	_____
_____	_____
_____	_____

Diagnosis:	Recheck:

Pet Behavior Journal

Veterinary Visit Journal
Date: _____

Reason for Visit:
_____
_____
_____
_____
_____
_____
_____

What Veterinarian said about my pet:
_____
_____
_____
_____
_____
_____
_____

Tests Done:	Medications:
_____	_____
_____	_____
_____	_____
_____	_____
_____	_____
Diagnosis:	Recheck:

Pet Behavior Journal

Veterinary Visit Journal

Date: _____

Reason for Visit:
_____
_____
_____
_____
_____
_____
_____

What Veterinarian said about my pet:
_____
_____
_____
_____
_____
_____
_____

Tests Done:
_____
_____
_____
_____
_____

Medications:
_____
_____
_____
_____
_____

Diagnosis:

Recheck:

Pet Behavior Journal

Veterinary Visit Journal
Date: _____

Reason for Visit:
_____
_____
_____
_____
_____
_____
_____

What Veterinarian said about my pet:
_____
_____
_____
_____
_____
_____
_____

Tests Done:	Medications:
_____	_____
_____	_____
_____	_____
_____	_____
_____	_____
_____	_____

Diagnosis:	Recheck:

Pet Behavior Journal

Veterinary Visit Journal
Date: _____

Reason for Visit:
_____
_____
_____
_____
_____
_____
_____
_____

What Veterinarian said about my pet:
_____
_____
_____
_____
_____
_____
_____
_____

Tests Done:
_____
_____
_____
_____
_____
_____

Medications:
_____
_____
_____
_____
_____
_____

Diagnosis:

Recheck:

Pet Behavior Journal

Veterinary Visit Journal
Date: _____

Reason for Visit:
_____
_____
_____
_____
_____
_____
_____
_____

What Veterinarian said about my pet:
_____
_____
_____
_____
_____
_____
_____
_____

Tests Done:	Medications:
_____	_____
_____	_____
_____	_____
_____	_____
_____	_____
Diagnosis:	**Recheck:**

Pet Behavior Journal

Veterinary Visit Journal
Date: _____

Reason for Visit:
_____
_____
_____
_____
_____
_____
_____

What Veterinarian said about my pet:
_____
_____
_____
_____
_____
_____
_____

Tests Done:	Medications:
_____	_____
_____	_____
_____	_____
_____	_____
_____	_____

Diagnosis:	Recheck:

Pet Behavior Journal

Veterinary Visit Journal
Date: _____

Reason for Visit:
_____
_____
_____
_____
_____
_____
_____

What Veterinarian said about my pet:
_____
_____
_____
_____
_____
_____
_____

Tests Done:
_____
_____
_____
_____
_____

Medications:
_____
_____
_____
_____
_____

Diagnosis:

Recheck:

Pet Behavior Journal

Veterinary Visit Journal
Date: _____

Reason for Visit:
_____
_____
_____
_____
_____
_____
_____

What Veterinarian said about my pet:
_____
_____
_____
_____
_____
_____
_____

Tests Done:
_____
_____
_____
_____
_____

Medications:
_____
_____
_____
_____
_____

Diagnosis:

Recheck:

Pet Behavior Journal

Veterinary Visit Journal
Date: _____

Reason for Visit:
_____
_____
_____
_____
_____
_____

What Veterinarian said about my pet:
_____
_____
_____
_____
_____
_____

Tests Done:
_____
_____
_____
_____
_____

Medications:
_____
_____
_____
_____
_____

Diagnosis:

Recheck:

Pet Behavior Journal

Veterinary Visit Journal

Date: _____

Reason for Visit:
_____
_____
_____
_____
_____
_____

What Veterinarian said about my pet:
_____
_____
_____
_____
_____
_____

Tests Done:	Medications:
_____	_____
_____	_____
_____	_____
_____	_____
_____	_____

Diagnosis:	Recheck:

Pet Behavior Journal

Veterinary Visit Journal
Date: _____

Reason for Visit:
_____
_____
_____
_____
_____
_____
_____

What Veterinarian said about my pet:
_____
_____
_____
_____
_____
_____
_____

Tests Done:
_____
_____
_____
_____
_____

Medications:
_____
_____
_____
_____
_____

Diagnosis:

Recheck:

Pet Behavior Journal

Veterinary Visit Journal
Date: _____

Reason for Visit:
_____
_____
_____
_____
_____
_____
_____

What Veterinarian said about my pet:
_____
_____
_____
_____
_____
_____
_____

Tests Done:
_____
_____
_____
_____
_____
_____

Medications:
_____
_____
_____
_____
_____
_____

Diagnosis:

Recheck:

Pet Behavior Journal

Veterinary Visit Journal
Date: _____

Reason for Visit:
_____
_____
_____
_____
_____
_____
_____

What Veterinarian said about my pet:
_____
_____
_____
_____
_____
_____
_____
_____

Tests Done:	Medications:
_____	_____
_____	_____
_____	_____
_____	_____
_____	_____

Diagnosis:	Recheck:

Pet Behavior Journal

Veterinary Visit Journal
Date: _____

Reason for Visit:
_____
_____
_____
_____
_____
_____

What Veterinarian said about my pet:
_____
_____
_____
_____
_____
_____

Tests Done:	Medications:
_____	_____
_____	_____
_____	_____
_____	_____
_____	_____

Diagnosis:	Recheck:

Pet Behavior Journal

Veterinary Visit Journal
Date: _____

Reason for Visit:
_____
_____
_____
_____
_____
_____
_____

What Veterinarian said about my pet:
_____
_____
_____
_____
_____
_____
_____

Tests Done:	Medications:
_____	_____
_____	_____
_____	_____
_____	_____
_____	_____

Diagnosis:	Recheck:

Pet Behavior Journal

Veterinary Visit Journal
Date: _____

Reason for Visit:
_____
_____
_____
_____
_____
_____
_____

What Veterinarian said about my pet:
_____
_____
_____
_____
_____
_____
_____

Tests Done:	Medications:
_____	_____
_____	_____
_____	_____
_____	_____
_____	_____

Diagnosis:	Recheck:

Pet Behavior Journal

Veterinary Visit Journal
Date: _____

Reason for Visit:
_____
_____
_____
_____
_____
_____
_____

What Veterinarian said about my pet:
_____
_____
_____
_____
_____
_____
_____
_____

Tests Done:	Medications:
_____	_____
_____	_____
_____	_____
_____	_____
_____	_____

Diagnosis:	Recheck:

Pet Behavior Journal

Veterinary Visit Journal
Date: _____

Reason for Visit:
_____
_____
_____
_____
_____
_____
_____

What Veterinarian said about my pet:
_____
_____
_____
_____
_____
_____
_____

Tests Done:	Medications:
_____	_____
_____	_____
_____	_____
_____	_____
_____	_____

Diagnosis:	Recheck:

Pet Behavior Journal

Veterinary Visit Journal
Date: _____

Reason for Visit:
_____
_____
_____
_____
_____
_____
_____

What Veterinarian said about my pet:
_____
_____
_____
_____
_____
_____
_____

Tests Done:	Medications:
_____	_____
_____	_____
_____	_____
_____	_____
_____	_____
Diagnosis:	**Recheck:**

Pet Behavior Journal

Veterinary Visit Journal
Date: _____

Reason for Visit:
_____
_____
_____
_____
_____
_____
_____

What Veterinarian said about my pet:
_____
_____
_____
_____
_____
_____
_____

Tests Done:	Medications:
_____	_____
_____	_____
_____	_____
_____	_____
_____	_____

Diagnosis:	Recheck:

Pet Behavior Journal

Veterinary Visit Journal
Date: _____

Reason for Visit:
_____
_____
_____
_____
_____
_____
_____

What Veterinarian said about my pet:
_____
_____
_____
_____
_____
_____
_____

Tests Done:
_____
_____
_____
_____
_____
_____

Medications:
_____
_____
_____
_____
_____
_____

Diagnosis:

Recheck:

Pet Behavior Journal

Veterinary Visit Journal

Date: _____

Reason for Visit:
_____
_____
_____
_____
_____
_____
_____

What Veterinarian said about my pet:
_____
_____
_____
_____
_____
_____
_____

Tests Done:
_____
_____
_____
_____
_____

Medications:
_____
_____
_____
_____
_____

Diagnosis:

Recheck:

Pet Behavior Journal

Veterinary Visit Journal

Date: _____

Reason for Visit:
_____
_____
_____
_____
_____
_____
_____

What Veterinarian said about my pet:
_____
_____
_____
_____
_____
_____
_____

Tests Done:
_____
_____
_____
_____
_____
_____

Medications:
_____
_____
_____
_____
_____
_____

Diagnosis:

Recheck:

Pet Behavior Journal

Veterinary Visit Journal
Date: _____

Reason for Visit:
_____
_____
_____
_____
_____
_____
_____

What Veterinarian said about my pet:
_____
_____
_____
_____
_____
_____
_____

Tests Done:	Medications:
_____	_____
_____	_____
_____	_____
_____	_____
_____	_____
Diagnosis:	**Recheck:**

Pet Behavior Journal

Veterinary Visit Journal
Date: _____

Reason for Visit:
_____
_____
_____
_____
_____
_____
_____

What Veterinarian said about my pet:
_____
_____
_____
_____
_____
_____
_____

Tests Done:
_____
_____
_____
_____
_____
_____

Medications:
_____
_____
_____
_____
_____
_____

Diagnosis:

Recheck:

Pet Behavior Journal

Veterinary Visit Journal
Date: _____

Reason for Visit:
_____
_____
_____
_____
_____
_____
_____
_____

What Veterinarian said about my pet:
_____
_____
_____
_____
_____
_____
_____
_____

Tests Done:	Medications:
_____	_____
_____	_____
_____	_____
_____	_____
_____	_____
_____	_____

Diagnosis:	Recheck:

Pet Behavior Journal

Veterinary Visit Journal
Date: _____

Reason for Visit:
_____
_____
_____
_____
_____
_____
_____

What Veterinarian said about my pet:
_____
_____
_____
_____
_____
_____
_____

Tests Done:	Medications:
_____	_____
_____	_____
_____	_____
_____	_____
_____	_____
_____	_____

Diagnosis:	Recheck:

Pet Behavior Journal

Veterinary Visit Journal
Date: _____

Reason for Visit:
_____
_____
_____
_____
_____
_____

What Veterinarian said about my pet:
_____
_____
_____
_____
_____
_____

Tests Done:	Medications:
_____	_____
_____	_____
_____	_____
_____	_____
_____	_____

Diagnosis:	Recheck:

Pet Behavior Journal

Veterinary Visit Journal
Date: _____

Reason for Visit:
_____
_____
_____
_____
_____
_____
_____

What Veterinarian said about my pet:
_____
_____
_____
_____
_____
_____
_____
_____

Tests Done:
_____
_____
_____
_____
_____

Medications:
_____
_____
_____
_____
_____

Diagnosis:

Recheck:

Pet Behavior Journal

Veterinary Visit Journal
Date: _____

Reason for Visit:
_____
_____
_____
_____
_____
_____

What Veterinarian said about my pet:
_____
_____
_____
_____
_____
_____

Tests Done:
_____
_____
_____
_____
_____
_____

Medications:
_____
_____
_____
_____
_____
_____

Diagnosis:

Recheck:

Pet Behavior Journal

Veterinary Visit Journal
Date: _____

Reason for Visit:
_____
_____
_____
_____
_____
_____
_____

What Veterinarian said about my pet:
_____
_____
_____
_____
_____
_____
_____

Tests Done:
_____
_____
_____
_____
_____
_____

Medications:
_____
_____
_____
_____
_____
_____

Diagnosis:

Recheck:

Pet Behavior Journal

Veterinary Visit Journal
Date: _____

Reason for Visit:
_____
_____
_____
_____
_____
_____
_____

What Veterinarian said about my pet:
_____
_____
_____
_____
_____
_____
_____

Tests Done:	**Medications:**
_____	_____
_____	_____
_____	_____
_____	_____
_____	_____
_____	_____

Diagnosis:	**Recheck:**

Pet Behavior Journal

Veterinary Visit Journal
Date: _____

Reason for Visit:
_____
_____
_____
_____
_____
_____
_____

What Veterinarian said about my pet:
_____
_____
_____
_____
_____
_____
_____

Tests Done:	Medications:
_____	_____
_____	_____
_____	_____
_____	_____
_____	_____

Diagnosis:	Recheck:

Pet Behavior Journal

Veterinary Visit Journal
Date: _____

Reason for Visit:
_____
_____
_____
_____
_____
_____
_____

What Veterinarian said about my pet:
_____
_____
_____
_____
_____
_____
_____
_____

Tests Done:
_____
_____
_____
_____
_____
_____

Medications:
_____
_____
_____
_____
_____
_____

Diagnosis:

Recheck:

Pet Behavior Journal

Veterinary Visit Journal
Date: _____

Reason for Visit:
_____
_____
_____
_____
_____
_____

What Veterinarian said about my pet:
_____
_____
_____
_____
_____
_____

Tests Done:	Medications:
_____	_____
_____	_____
_____	_____
_____	_____

Diagnosis:	Recheck:

Pet Behavior Journal

Veterinary Visit Journal
Date: _____

Reason for Visit:
_____
_____
_____
_____
_____
_____
_____

What Veterinarian said about my pet:
_____
_____
_____
_____
_____
_____
_____

Tests Done:
_____
_____
_____
_____
_____
_____

Medications:
_____
_____
_____
_____
_____
_____

Diagnosis:

Recheck:

Pet Behavior Journal

Pet Behavior Journal

www.ingramcontent.com/pod-product-compliance
Lightning Source LLC
Chambersburg PA
CBHW022215180225
22178CB00008B/246